[CODING_CAREERS] for Tomorrow

CODING CAREERS IN MANUFACTURING

Kaitlyn Duling

Cavendish Square
New York

Published in 2020 by Cavendish Square Publishing, LLC
243 5th Avenue, Suite 136, New York, NY 10016

First Edition

Website: cavendishsq.com

Library of Congress Cataloging-in-Publication Data

Names: Duling, Kaitlyn, author.
Title: Coding careers in manufacturing / Kaitlyn Duling.
Description: First edition. | New York, NY : Cavendish Square Publishing, LLC, 2020. | Series: Coding careers for tomorrow | Includes bibliographical references and index. | Audience: Grades 7 to 12. Identifiers: LCCN 2018060540 (print) | LCCN 2019000668 (ebook) | ISBN 9781502645869 (ebook) | ISBN 9781502645852 (library bound) | ISBN 9781502645845 (pbk.)
Subjects: LCSH: Production engineering–Data processing–Vocational guidance–Juvenile literature. | Manufacturing processes–Data processing–Vocational guidance–Juvenile literature. | Computer programming–Juvenile literature.Classification: LCC TS155.6 (ebook) | LCC TS155.6 .D85 2020 (print) | DDC 670.285–dc23
LC record available at https://lccn.loc.gov/2018060540

Editorial Director: David McNamara
Editor: Kristen Susienka
Copy Editor: Denise Larrabee
Associate Art Director: Alan Sliwinski
Designer: Ginny Kemmerer
Production Coordinator: Karol Szymczuk
Photo Research: J8 Media

The photographs in this book are used by permission and through the courtesy of:
Cover PaO Studio/Shutterstock.com, Maciek905/iStockphoto.com (used throughout); p. 4 Hero Images/Getty Images; p. 6 Gerenme/Getty Images; p. 8 New York Public Library/Interim Archives/Getty Images; p. 9 Gerhard Joren/Light Rocket/Getty Images; p. 10 Tim Rue/Bloomberg/Getty Images, MF3d/iStockphoto.com (used throughout); p. 12 Geoff Caddick/AFP/Getty Images; p. 15 Thomas Allom/Getty Images; p. 17 Iain Masterton/Alamy Stock Photo; p. 20 Westend61/Getty Images; p. 24 Stockfour/Shutterstock.com; p. 28 Hadrian/Shutterstock.com; p. 31 Garn Phakathunya/Alamy Stock Photo; p. 34 Francois Nascimbeni/AFP/Getty Images; p. 37 Halfpoint/Shutterstock.com; p. 39 Jens Kalaene/Picture Alliance/Getty Images; p. 42 Sean Zero Three/iStockphoto.com; p. 46 BSIP/UIG/Getty Images; p. 48 Michael Duva/Getty Images; p. 51 Digital First Media/Orange County Register/Getty Images; p. 53 Skynesher/Getty Images; p. 54 Ann Hermes/Christian Science Monitor/The Image Works; p. 56 Roberto E. Rosales/Albuquerque Journal/ZUMA Wire/Alamy Stock Photo; p. 58 Joe Amon/The Denver Post/Getty Images; p. 60 Andresr/iStock/Getty Images; p. 64 Toru Hanai/REUTERS/Newscom.

Printed in the United States of America

Contents

chapter_01 Caution: Coders at Work! 5

chapter_02 Fully Automated 13

chapter_03 Innovative Technologies 29

chapter_04 A Coding Career 43

chapter_05 Get Coding 55

Glossary 66

Further Information 69

Bibliography 72

Index 78

About the Author 80

Digital tools—from laptops and smartphones to virtual reality—all depend on the work of coders.

chapter_01

Caution: Coders at Work!

"Buzz … buzz … buzz …" When your phone vibrates in the middle of dinner (or class!), you might be receiving a text message, getting a notification from an application, or missing a video call. These interactions happen to most people several times—maybe even hundreds of times—a day. When you get a free moment, you'll contact your friends, check your apps, and send emails. These might be simple items on your digital to-do list, but each and every thing you do on your smartphone or on the internet has been created through code.

Codes are the languages that help make software, websites, and applications (or apps). Web browsers and social media networks are created with code. Today, everything from shoe factories to electrical plants utilize some type of code. The twenty-first century is a digital one. In a short time, coders have mastered the languages that are being used to build our world. There is a vital need for more coders in the workforce today. Coders have the opportunity to write new programs, create apps, and even make products come to life.

CODING WORKS

When considering the sophisticated robots and machines of the last couple decades, it is important to remember that these computerized wonders don't control themselves. Machines that incorporate computers into their processes still need humans to give them directions. At its most basic,

Today's factories utilize robots to do advanced processes. In this factory, robots manufacture the body of a vehicle.

that's what coding is: giving directions to computers. A coder can tell a computer to display a certain word or picture on a website. A coder can also teach a machine to pour *just* the right amount of chocolate into candy molds, producing thousands of pieces each hour.

Those who code as a career are oftentimes referred to as programmers or developers, especially when they are writing code for software. Coders learn computer languages in order to give directions to specific machines and types of computers. These languages aren't the Spanish and German that you learn in high school. Today's popular coding languages have names like Java, Ruby, C++, and Python. Many are made up of complex letter, number, and symbol patterns. Others use pictures and shapes. Programming languages are taught in schools, colleges, and special bootcamps that get you up to speed in a short amount of time. For those who want to become fluent in the language of computers, there are plenty of options.

THE FIRST CODERS

You might think that the history of coding only goes back a few years, or even a couple decades. However, it can actually be traced all the way back to the 1800s! Between 1842 and 1843, a woman named Ada Lovelace translated the memoir of an Italian scientist named Francis Maneclang. His book shared the details of a new machine called the analytical

This illustration shows Ada Lovelace, a pioneer among women in STEM as well as one of the first programmers.

engine. Along with her translation, Lovelace added notes for a new algorithm that would work on what was, essentially, a computer. Sadly, the engine was never built. Though her algorithm was never tested, many consider this pioneering woman's algorithm to be the very first programming language.

The codes we recognize today as closer to our present-day programming languages popped up nearly one hundred years later, in the 1950s and 1960s, alongside early machines and computers. While there is much dispute over which contemporary language was introduced first, one of the earliest high-level languages was called FORTRAN, which stood for "Formula Translation." FORTRAN was invented in 1954 by a team of coders at IBM. Compared to the old means of programming computers, FORTRAN's code was straightforward, relatively simple, and very efficient. In fact, it was so ahead of its time that the language is still used by some computers today.

CODING AND MANUFACTURING

Throughout the 1960s, more and better programming languages were introduced. Still, they were fairly basic by today's standards. As the years passed, the languages were put to use on more than one computer at a time, and then they expanded to include whole computer systems. By the 1990s, programmers were ready for the internet. Access to the personal computer and the internet boomed in the

Cars have long been manufactured on assembly lines. Today, robots stand on either side of the conveyor belt, rather than humans.

THE EVOLUTION OF AUTOCAD

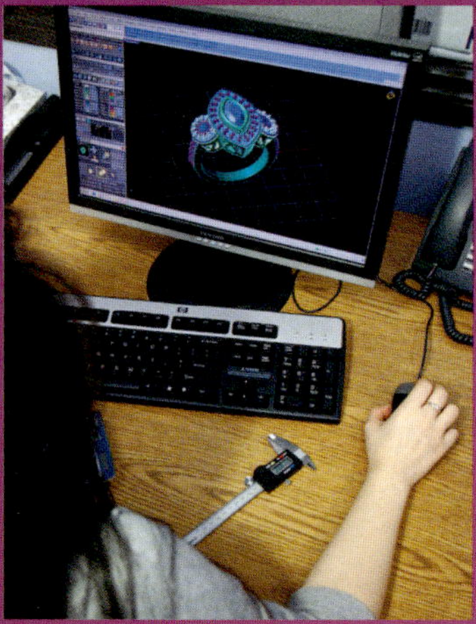

CAD programs can be accessed on desktops, laptops, tablets, and even smartphones.

One of the most widely used programs in the manufacturing and design sectors is AutoCAD. Before AutoCAD, designs were drawn with pen and paper. Today, AutoCAD software lets designers, architects, and others create technical drawings and simulations. Did an architect design AutoCAD? Nope—a coder did! In fact, a team of around fifteen developers came together to found a company called Autodesk in 1982. A man named John Walker spearheaded the group. Together, the group hoped to come up with five different applications. They collected just $60,000 and agreed to work without pay for one year. The group ended up putting their collective investment and hard work into one program: AutoCAD, which launched that same year at the COMDEX trade show in Las Vegas. The computer-aided design (CAD) program was the first of its kind to run on a personal computer. It took off! AutoCAD became profitable almost immediately. Since its release, there have been over thirty versions of the program, and it remains popular year after year.

mid-1990s, giving coders an entirely new stage for their work. Since then, the world of programming languages has continued to expand quickly, and coders are discovering new and inventive ways to use the languages that exist. One industry that has embraced coding as a necessity in the last few years is manufacturing.

At their core, programming languages are designed for several different functions: designing web pages, solving math problems, running analytic programs, making desktop software, running apps, and more. What makes the twenty-first century so different? We have finally entered a period in the digital age when computer languages not only tell machines what to do on a screen, but directly influence things that happen in real life, such as a robotic machine building a product, or a software system alerting a factory to new inventory that will be produced the next day. Just like the very first websites, today's 3D printers and robots need programmers to tell them what to do. This has turned out to be a great fit for the manufacturing industry, which makes all of the "stuff" we need, want, buy, or sell. Without manufacturing, we wouldn't have any stuff. Without coders, manufacturing (and thus, our stuff!) would look much different than it does today.

This factory floor in the United Kingdom uses robotic arms to build BMW Mini vehicles. The floor is empty of people.

chapter_02

Fully Automated

Since the rise of computers, the internet, and coding, American factories have been growing and changing. Today, they don't look much like their historical predecessors, which took shape about two hundred years ago. To say that coders have had a small impact on the manufacturing industry is a massive understatement, for they have truly shaped how numerous objects are produced, from clothing to automobiles to food products. Coding and programming professionals affect almost every step in the manufacturing process. From a product's creation to its final sale in retail stores or online, coders are continuously changing and improving the process.

FROM THE 1800s TO TODAY

To fully grasp the effects that coding professionals have had on the manufacturing industry, one must first examine the origins of manufacturing in the United States. The discovery of coal power and the creation of machine production worked together to mark the 1820s as the dawn of industry in the United States. The Industrial Revolution transformed everything about "making." Instead of an artisan making one musket at a time, a machine could spend all day producing the parts for many muskets. The next day it would make the next part, and so on, until there were cases of muskets that could be sold to the public. Automobiles, tools, and other products followed suit. The race to produce products—lots of them—had begun.

For decades, factories used machines to produce goods, but relied on workers to run the machines and to complete essential tasks that machines could not do. For example, in a textile factory, a mechanized loom would weave beautiful fabrics, but workers had to be present to switch out new spools of thread whenever one was emptied. Workers checked for errors, turned machines off at the end of the day, and packed items for shipment. People and machines worked together. For many years, the American manufacturing industry remained robust, with jobs available for those who wanted to commit to long days at the factory. Humans decided what was made, crunched the numbers, and

One of the earliest factory advancements was the power loom, used in textile factories, which was introduced in 1785. This engraving shows people working in a power loom factory in the 1830s.

analyzed what was purchased in stores. This is key—at the time, *everything* was purchased in stores or through catalogs in the mail. The world was not yet online.

Starting in the 1970s, the tide began to change. Remember, new programming languages were being introduced in the 1950s and 1960s, and computers were slowly gaining popularity, especially in business. In 1973, two companies, ABB Robotics and KUKA Robotics, spearheaded the creation of industrial robots, which were meant to work in factories. These were embraced and adopted by US companies as quickly as possible, for robots could do accurate work within a controlled window of time. Robots are predictable, reliable, and manageable. Unlike humans, technology is never late for work; doesn't ask for vacation days; and never gets the flu.

In the middle of all of this robot creation came the peak of employment in the American manufacturing industry. According to data published by the Bureau of Labor Statistics, employment in this industry soared in 1979. This was a time when many factories were open. They had products to make, and they needed lots of people in order to meet the demand. Soon after this employment peak, technology began to speed up. Personal computers became popular, clearing the way for computers to enter factories on an even more frequent basis. Additionally, digital RFID (radio-frequency identification) technology tags were invented in 1983. These small labels made it easier to tag and identify things using mobile readers. Factories were finally becoming automated.

The early industrial robots that began to appear in factories could do basic assembly jobs, welding, and object movement. Many of them looked like large metal arms that could grasp items. Controlled by computers (which were programmed by humans), the robots evolved in the 1980s and 1990s. They could work faster and smarter, making them more productive. By the 2000s, robots were part of many American factories. Not only that, but the internet had made an appearance in factories too—on the factory floor and in the boardroom. Other areas also began to house computers with internet capabilities—offices, stores, and even customers' homes. The rise of the internet in the manufacturing industry has completely changed the ways in which goods are designed, produced, and purchased. Today, programmers are front and center when it comes to all three parts of the manufacturing industry.

DESIGNING STUFF

When we think of the term "manufacturing," we usually think of making something—pouring plastic into molds, welding car parts together, and cutting pieces of furniture to be stacked into kits for sale. However, before objects can be made for human consumption, they first need to go through a design process. Unsurprisingly, today coding is part of this

This engineer uses a CAD application on a tablet to design a bridge. Mobile technology helps designers build models on the go.

process. In fact, it was one of the first manufacturing aspects to be touched by the power of programming.

In the 1950s, computer scientists at Massachusetts Institute of Technology (MIT) and other universities were hard at work designing programs that would meet the needs of designers, architects, engineers, and others who needed models. When a company is preparing itself to produce a new product, be it a palm-sized fidget spinner or a four-door car, it first needs to create a model. Decades ago, models were drawn using pencil and paper. Think of an antique drafting table, or an architect bent low beneath a light bulb, sketching. Clay and cardboard were used too. It wasn't until the post–World War II era that people began to spend time and brain power creating engineering drawings with computers.

In 1957, Dr. Patrick J. Hanratty was developing PRONTO (Program for Numerical Tooling Operations), a commercial programming system. Among scholars, Hanratty is often referred to as the "father of CAD." CAD is the process of designing models on a computer. One might use a CAD program to draw a 2D model of a motorcycle. Six different drawings would give the designer a view of each side. Alternatively, one could also use a CAD program to draw a 3D model of the same motorcycle, which would give a complete, 360-degree perspective of the object. CAD software like SketchUp and AutoCAD are used by hobbyists who want to create original designs, but they are also used by manufacturers during product planning. Who codes those software systems? Coders! Great design software relies on great coders who understand the wants and needs of companies.

Coders are also needed when it comes to designing machines, robots, software, and applications. After a product has been developed, a team has to figure out how it will be built. Will it be made by hand? For objects produced at a large scale, probably not. Will it be made on an assembly line, with humans adding parts at different intervals? Again, probably not. An assembly line might still be used, but it will probably be composed of a combination of humans and automated machines or robots. A new product might even be 3D-printed by a machine, with no human worker necessary during the process itself. Skilled humans are needed when it comes to programming the printer, robots, and other machines. As intelligent as we have made them, even robots lack the minds to make organic, creative designs. It's up to coders to figure out the software that will be needed in order to make machines work.

MAKING STUFF

Once a product has been designed, it moves on to the next phase, production. Thanks to skilled coders, there are now numerous options when it comes to producing an object efficiently. As we've learned, the manufacturing industry

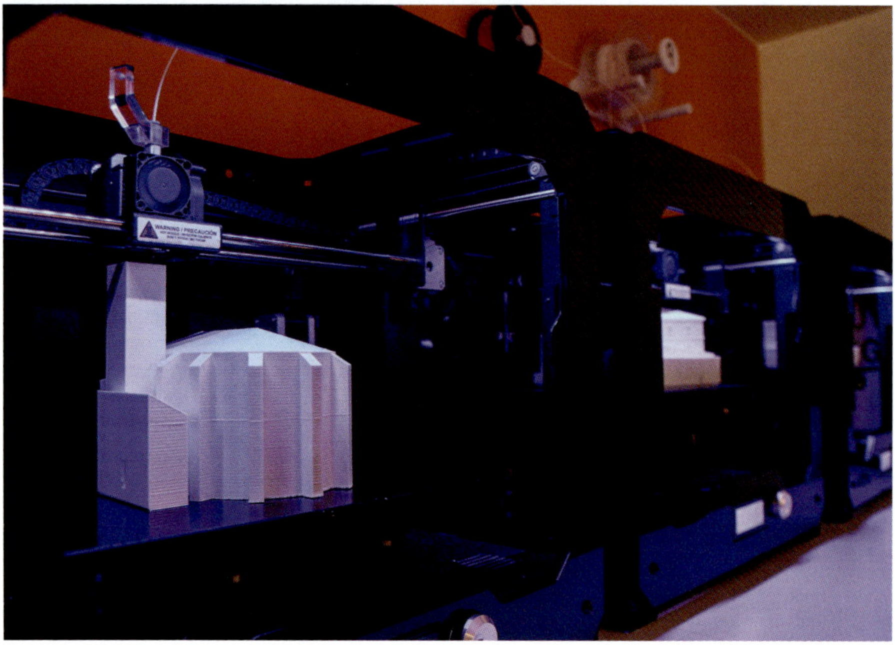

Among other things, a 3D printer can create scale models of buildings, such as the one this 3D printer is making.

has changed a lot over the past few decades. While human workers are still around, they aren't doing quite the same work they were just a few years ago. Instead of welding and carrying power tools, today's factory workers are sitting at desks, developing software, and programming automated machines. Even those who operate machines on the factory floor are working with technology so advanced that the work requires years of training before one can stand next to the assembly line. It seems that technology has taken over the factory floor, and workers must now keep up.

If humans aren't producing goods ... what is? The answer involves robots, assembly lines, machines, printers, lasers, and so much more. Before we dive into the newest innovations in manufacturing, it's important to get a handle on one principle: computer-aided manufacturing. Today's large-scale manufacturing machines, whether they are technically robotic or not, are connected to computers. Factories are equipped with Wi-Fi that allows workers to program and track production in real time. Once a CAD program has been used to design a new sneaker, the model and specifications can be uploaded to one of any number of advanced machines. With the right inputs and tools, the machine can build a shoe. And another. And another! Mostly absent of human workers, production floors are becoming more efficient. They can work at any hour and on any day, even on holidays.

One of the simplest examples of technologically advanced production is the rise of the 3D printer. These machines were first developed in the 1980s, but they have only become affordable and widespread in the 2000s. A 3D printer uses a 3D model (like one you might make on AutoCAD or another software program) to create a three-dimensional object. A material like plastic is added to the printer, which then melts and binds together, layer by layer, to build the object. Usually this happens from the bottom up. At first, these machines were just used to make tiny plastic figurines

Negative Impact

The story has played out many times, in towns big and small across the United States and Canada. Many communities have had one or two anchor, or longtime, factories since sometime in the twentieth century, and some companies even stretch back to the nineteenth century, when they opened up their first industrial centers. Unfortunately, because of rapid technological advancements in the industry, as well as the movement of production to other countries in order to lower costs, many of these anchor factories have closed. What sounds like a natural occurrence can feel like a devastating loss within a community, especially when hundreds (or even thousands) of local workers are left without jobs.

In these cases, coding has had a negative impact on local communities and workers. Those whose primary responsibilities on the factory floor were manual labor can find it challenging to be retrained to fit new roles. A worker who spent decades of his or her life working with his or her hands must now utilize very specific parts of his or her brain in order to solve complex programming issues. Those coding jobs might come with better pay and fewer accidents and injuries, but they are not open to all workers who have been displaced by technology.

and shapes. But now the technology has advanced enough to be used commercially. Everything from car parts and medical devices to sneakers and dinnerware are being 3D printed. The process is usually performed entirely within the machine itself, needing no humans other than coders. Programmers build the software, code the system, and even write programs that can observe, analyze, and make adjustments during and after the printing takes place. When it comes to production, today's coders are indispensable.

SELLING STUFF

Coders are involved in almost every aspect of modern manufacturing. They build software for modeling, they program the machines that build products, and so much more. One might assume that a coder's job stops once the products have been created. When the sneakers are in the box and ready to ship, it's time for the coders in the room to move on—but wait! The manufacturing industry has become so reliant on technology that skilled coders are needed every step of the way, from first idea to delivery of the product into the consumer's hands.

Automation and advanced technology have led to major increases in competition between manufacturers. Their processes are more efficient and cost-effective, and it is much easier to create quick prototypes, or mock objects, to test before sending a giant order to the factory. This increase in competition means that companies have been forced to become even more savvy than ever before. It's not enough to dream up a great product, build a million of them, and then sell it. With so many brands crowding the marketplace, consumer choices and tastes are changing constantly. What's a competitive brand to do? It gets smart. It takes a deep dive into analysis.

One of the biggest ways that coders have helped move the manufacturing industry forward has been through analytical processes. Coders are writing all sorts of software,

For those who love to work on computers and tablets, a coding career can be a satisfying and comfortable fit.

POSITIVE IMPACT

With the downturn in labor jobs and the increase in coding positions, there have been great challenges—but also significant hope. Worker-retraining programs are one option that has proven successful for some unemployed factory workers. Today, companies like Amazon, Google, and Microsoft are offering career-training programs to attract those left jobless due to automation. Their courses and programs are training workers in information technology, cybersecurity, and other skills that are in higher demand as industries get automated. Programs have been created through community colleges, universities, and even local libraries in order to retrain these large parts of the workforce. Some are retrained in computer programming, while others pursue office administration, construction work, and other new career paths that may or may not be related to their original job. Communities, states, and entire regions are rallying together to make sure that their workforce is retrained—and rehired.

Additionally, upon leaving the factory floor, many retrained workers find that their new positions, whether they are in or outside a factory, are much safer. Manufacturing has been rife with workplace injuries due to large machinery, repetitive movements, noisy conditions, and dangerous parts. A switch from the factory floor to the office cubicle can be difficult, but for many people, it offers a healthy and much needed change.

Coders work with many types of computer languages to create different innovative programs.

applications, and programs that can use data to create helpful reports. One software program might collect and organize data about consumer responses to a commercial. Another might track exactly which style of jeans is being purchased the most. Yet another program can be used to analyze the speed of a 3D printer throughout a time period, or the number of times a robot needed to be adjusted by a technician during a day. Before, these types of detailed analyses were only available through endless human observation and lots of arithmetic. However, this is no longer the case. Coders are not only able to write programs that collect and organize data, but they can code those programs to make automatic changes to factory machines. Yes—an application running on a tablet can tell a factory worker everything they need to know about the production happening on the floor, and with just the swipe of a finger, it can direct the robotic arms to twist left instead of right. It can slow and stop an assembly line. And more.

While we will get deeper into this interconnected web of technology a little later, a key point to note is that all of this coding work is not only making manufacturing faster and more efficient, but it is making it smarter. So instead of cutting costs by simply producing more, companies are also saving when they can use analytical software that tells them exactly how many of their products they should produce, or when they should be produced, or even (amazingly) what people want them to produce. While the CEO of a manufacturing company might be in charge, it is the skilled coder who is calling the shots behind the scenes, figuring out what needs to happen and developing the best way to do it.

Smartphones are examples of how far technology has advanced in just a matter of decades—all thanks to coders.

chapter_03

Innovative Technologies

Think back to the first time you used a computer or an application on your phone. Chances are, the technology looked different from the websites and apps you use today. Technology is something that is always changing and evolving. This means that coders need to change too! Throughout their careers, computer programmers keep learning about their field and improving their skills. From tiny changes to huge advancements that transform the face of the industry, the evolution is always in progress. Over the last few years, there have been a few major tech innovations that are shaping the manufacturing industry. As always, coders have increased their knowledge in order to keep up with the innovations and to make them better. In many ways, coders are designing the future.

ARTIFICIAL INTELLIGENCE

One arena that has completely transformed the field of manufacturing is artificial intelligence, or AI. This refers to intelligence inside machines and computers. It includes robots and other advanced machines that can do many of the same things humans can do. Decades ago, when they were first introduced, robotic arms and other AI-enabled machines could perform simple tasks like welding and picking up things. Today, their purpose has expanded beyond monotonous tasks. With advanced machine vision, robots can do maintenance on equipment in real time, using cameras to catch the slightest errors and logging what needs to be fixed. Usually, the robots can also do the fixing. This is known as predictive maintenance. Using smart sensors that see, hear, and pick up on vibrations, the robots know immediately when a machine is not functioning properly. It saves both time and money, and ensures that machines are always working at their peak performance. AI can also be used to notify teams when subtle production issues threaten the quality of a product. While a human can look at and touch an object coming down an assembly line, robots can often predict issues before they happen and step in to prevent them.

Some robots are designed to look (and act!) like humans, with "eyes," "arms," and more. This industrial robot is working in a computer manufacturing company.

AI is also being used further along the supply chain. Manufacturers always hope to respond to customer demand as quickly as possible in order to make money and cut costs. In this arena, artificial intelligence can help, even if it doesn't involve robots. Today, algorithms can look for patterns in demand across time, markets, locations, and population segments. When they do notice patterns and take things into account—weather, time of year, costs—these intelligent programs can suggest changes in production output and even seamlessly send those changes to the robots on the factory floor. This is a major example of machine intelligence that doesn't necessarily include a robotic feature. Artificial intelligence is all about teaching machines and robots to work intelligently, and that can take many forms.

CLOUD COMPUTING

You may have already heard of the cloud. This is a giant space online where information is stored. Anyone can store material on it. You can store your music and pictures in the cloud. It is also changing the way companies store and organize their information. For many manufacturing companies, other parts of their operation—factories, offices, and headquarters—might be spread out across the country, and even across the world. With cloud computing, every person, machine, and robot can share information—wherever they are. Data is managed and processed remotely. Those who work with data might not even need to leave their house! Cloud computing is helping companies make better, more efficient, and more cost-effective business decisions, and it is helping increase both access and transparency among workers.

In the long term, cloud computing can even reduce production times on products. Because information is shared instantly and decisions are made quickly, factories can switch almost immediately from producing one product to making a similar one, or tweaking the original in some way. As cloud computing networks become more popular, and as coders work to make them even better, we can expect to see companies churning out more products and more customizable options.

INTERNET OF THINGS

What do we mean when we say "smart" manufacturing? Think about the ways in which your smartphone can connect to other technology inside your home. You might use it to turn up the volume on your television, check the temperature inside the oven, or change the brightness of lights in your house. In popular language, this connectedness is referred to as the Internet of Things, or IoT. The Internet of Things isn't just giving us smart speakers with voices and video cameras for our dogs. It's also changing the way we manufacture goods.

Facilities themselves have become smart. On modern factory floors, you can see workers controlling machines via tablets and phones. When machines and robots are connected over the internet, they can communicate with each other, and humans can communicate with them. Gone are the days in which a person had to flip a switch to turn on the lights in a factory, then touch a button to turn on a machine and manage the settings in a fan to keep the machine cool.

Instead of human actions, all of these things can be programmed far in advance, and monitored via smart applications. When issues are detected, all aspects of production can be notified, changed, and even halted. It is the hope that the IoT will mean less downtime for machines, more detailed control over work in factories, less waste, and lower costs overall.

NANOTECHNOLOGY

For this innovation, you need to think small. *Really* small. Nanotechnology is a type of tech that deals with matter up to 100 nanometers in size. How big is a nanometer? One-billionth of a meter! A meter is about 3 feet long. Can you picture something one billion times smaller? For a long time, nanotechnology has played a big role in the medical field—helping scientists study extremely small cells and bacteria in

3D printing isn't done with plastic alone. The parts this man is holding were printed using hot, liquid metal. They are examples of printed medical parts.

order to improve our health. Technology of this scale is also used in aerospace engineering, where the science needs to be exact, down to the smallest detail, in order to create a safe, lightweight, powerful spaceship or airplane.

Now, nanotechnology is moving into the manufacturing industry. It is being used to create high-tech materials that are strong and lightweight. Some examples include lightweight tennis rackets that have improved players' hitting power, and fishing rods that are strong yet light. Computer chips, computer memory devices, thin saw blades, and solar cells have all experienced advancements in nanotechnology that make them faster, stronger, and better for consumers.

ADDITIVE MANUFACTURING

We already know that 3D printing is becoming a popular tool in the manufacturing sphere. But 3D printing is actually part of a larger umbrella term called additive manufacturing, or AM. This refers to any technology that builds objects by adding layers of material. This can be done with layers of plastic, layers of concrete, layers of metal, and other materials. Some people even believe that someday we will be able to use additive manufacturing with human tissues in order to create replacement body parts. Whoa! That's probably a long way off, but maybe not entirely out of the realm of possibility.

AM is not only used to produce objects on a large scale. It is also used to rapidly create prototypes. If you are thinking about making a new type of sneaker, you would first need a prototype. It might not be exactly like the final product, but it gives people an idea of the sneaker you want to eventually produce and sell. The prototyping process used to take a long time, but advancements in coding and tech mean that prototypes can now be created quickly. This allows products to get to market faster.

What are we using AM for right now? Some of its most popular applications include small auto parts and fashion products. A hair clip or piece of jewelry might be made using this type of technology, or a cap that fits on an engine. Aerospace companies are particularly interested in AM, as this tech is ideal for producing parts that are both light and strong. AM is also used for things that are simple but plentiful in the market. Additionally, AM is being used in the medical world. Through the use of computer-aided design software, medical designers can make dental implants that fit their patients perfectly. Then they can use additive manufacturing to produce the tooth from the bottom up, building it to suit the individual.

AUTONOMOUS VEHICLES

Self-driving cars are one of today's most popular ideas. Companies from Google to Uber are in a race to design a road-ready car that can drive itself. However, this is not the only role that autonomous vehicles will perform in the

Some companies are testing the use of drones for picking up and moving goods inside large warehouses.

future. While someday we may be able to hop into a car that drives us to the movie theater, there will also be self-driving vehicles on factory floors, moving in between robots, intelligent machines, and workers carrying tablets.

In a factory setting, there aren't usually cars driving around, but there are vehicles. Oftentimes these are forklifts or other human-driven vehicles that lift pallets full of products and move them from one place to another. After they are built, goods will eventually move on to a distribution center, and from there they will move to businesses or direct to consumers' homes. Autonomous vehicles will be involved in all of this movement, from trucking goods between distribution centers and businesses to moving items around the factory floor. Some warehouses are already using drone-like robotic "pickers" that drive around the warehouse, find the objects that have been ordered, and then deliver the goods to a human, who prepares them for shipment. Amazon has been innovative in this respect, and now other companies are doing the same and working hard to perfect the system.

All of this automated movement isn't meant to displace humans on the job. Autonomous vehicles are making factories and warehouses safer places, as they use data and intelligent cameras to reduce accidents and injuries. They can also work faster and more reliably than humans, decreasing waste and making processes more efficient.

AUGMENTED AND VIRTUAL REALITY

One innovation that is still in its earliest stages of development for manufacturing is mixed reality. Mixed reality includes both virtual and augmented reality technologies. You may have heard of virtual reality, or VR, especially when it comes to video games that cover your eyes and ears, putting you in the game, and making everything you perceive seem real. Augmented reality, or AR, combines elements of virtual technology with things that are truly seen and heard.

In manufacturing, workers are used to dealing with the real environment. To operate machines, they use dials, buttons, and physical screens. In the future, augmented reality might allow a factory worker to put on a pair of special glasses that helps them see digital instructions for assembly at the same time they are seeing and assembling a physical part. These screens appear to float in the air and can be controlled through voice commands, freeing up a worker's hands to focus on the task. The carmaker Volvo has been testing similar AR processes in recent years.

In addition to providing AR screens for workers on the assembly line, virtual reality is being used for design purposes. Someday, high-end interior designers and architects might utilize VR systems to let customers "walk" through a design plan for their house before it has been physically transformed or built. Meanwhile, companies might use VR to walk through their factory floors before they have been built, inspecting

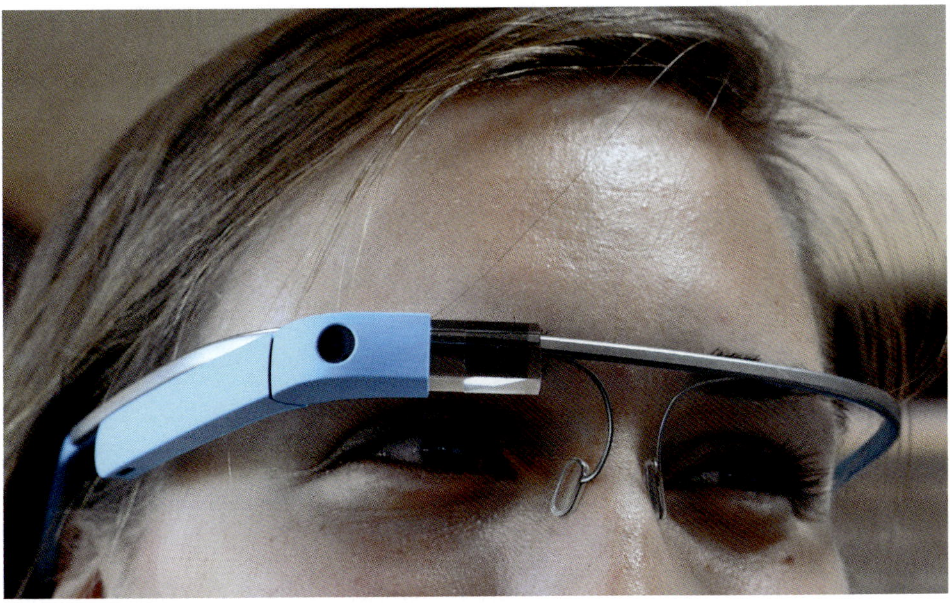

Google Glass featured a tiny computer attached to the frame. It was an attempt at AR for the everyday consumer. Unfortunately, it didn't sell very well and Google abandoned the product.

Generative Design

One new technology that has turned the manufacturing industry upside down is generative design. This new technology is being led by CAD software companies like Autodesk that have roots in design programs.

In a traditional CAD program, like AutoCAD, a designer can make a design and then tweak it many times. Generative design takes out the guesswork. It utilizes elements of cloud computing and intelligent machinery to provide designers with solutions. Generative design programs, such as Autodesk's Fusion 360, allow a designer to input goals such as costs, materials, and method of manufacturing. Then the software program finds thousands of different solutions. From there, the software can also test these options, learn from them, and offer alternatives. It is an incredibly fast and accurate way to not only build better products but to figure out the most cost-effective, efficient, and desirable ways to do so.

everything from safety options to efficient layouts that could improve their processes. More than a simple model, VR allows people to experience things before they are built. In the world of manufacturing, where new factories and production lines have large budgets, VR and AR could prove themselves to be very valuable.

Some coders work in offices, while others work at home or on the road.

chapter_04

A Coding Career

Now that we know what coding looks like on a practical level and have seen the innovation that can be achieved by computer programmers working in the manufacturing industry, where does that leave workers? Those considering a career in coding for the manufacturing industry should not despair, for they have many options and opportunities.

EARLY CAREERS

At one time in US history, factories were a secure, reliable, and profitable source of employment. In the early twentieth century, it was common for young men to get jobs in manufacturing and keep them until retirement, perhaps moving up the ranks until they managed groups of workers on the factory floor, oversaw safety regulations, or even helped design new processes. During World War II, women were given the opportunity to join the manufacturing industry in large numbers. With their husbands away at war, women needed to earn money, and wartime equipment needed to be produced. The icon "Rosie the Riveter" was created during World War II as a symbol of the strong women who took jobs in factories. The figure was an example of the physical nature of the job. Rosie needed to be tough. She even had to put her hair up in a handkerchief! That's how physically demanding the factories were at the time.

Today's manufacturing sector looks different from what it did in the 1940s. Sure, some products are still crafted by hand, and some need humans on the assembly line to do things like packaging, quality control, and final touches. However, many factory floor jobs have been replaced by robotic elements, also called automation. Many people are concerned that automation is hurting job prospects in the manufacturing industry, but that is only partially true. There may be fewer traditional jobs, such as riveting or welding, but the market for computer programmers and engineers is booming.

JOB OUTLOOK

As students graduate college and move into the workforce, experts predict that there will be many jobs available for coders in the manufacturing industry. Moreover, these jobs will offer security and prosperity. Computer-oriented jobs have always paid well, and coding is no exception. Someone who is an expert in one or more computer languages can expect to make salaries ranging from $50,000 to over three figures, depending on their experience in the field and the location of the job. Some jobs are done on-site at company headquarters or within a factory itself, while others can be done remotely. This is especially true as cloud computing and automation become more common. Information technology professionals don't necessarily need to be on-site to tackle technological issues. Much of the work can be done from anywhere in the world, as long as there is a secure internet connection.

In many ways, it will be easier for those who wish to pursue a career in manufacturing to enter the job market with a coding or computer science background. Manufacturing is moving toward technological solutions in nearly every step of the design, production, and analysis processes. Consider specifically the new innovations discussed earlier—nanotechnology, for example—the innovative processes that surround working on ever smaller scales and rely heavily on machines and computers. Coders will need to write the programs that deal with nanotechnology, and there will be other opportunities for further creativity and innovation within that field.

Additionally, artificial intelligence and robotics are going to need computer programmers who are interested in machine learning (ML), the processes by which we can "teach" machines and make them more "intelligent" or capable of solving problems with multiple options. Programmers use computer languages to teach machines. In the manufacturing industry, more companies are looking for machines that work intelligently and autonomously. Coders will be some of the most important players in this field.

When looking for jobs, those wanting a coding career will not go directly to the doors of factories or the websites of specific manufacturers to find work. Prospective coders within the manufacturing industry will most likely choose a specialty. Areas of interest can be chosen in college,

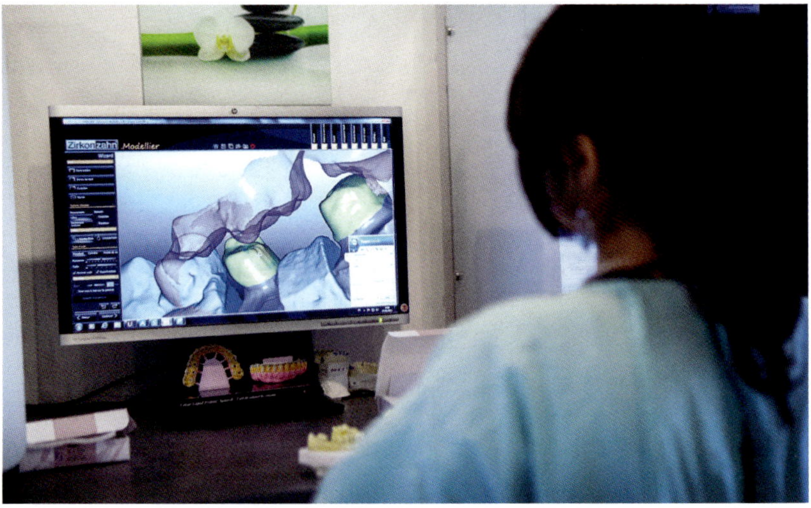

The medical industry utilizes coders to help create programs, models, and even robots that do surgery! This medical lab uses a CAD system to take a 3D image from dental impression scans.

coding bootcamp, or even when reading and practicing coding outside of traditional pathways. A coder interested in manufacturing could specialize in computer-aided design and generative design; robotics; machine–human interaction and machine learning; or 3D printing. Then, he or she would search for jobs within that specialization. Instead of working at one company for many decades, coders often bounce between companies, gathering knowledge and experience along the way. Especially if one is interested in innovation and creativity, it makes sense to follow companies that are doing new and inventive work.

Alternatively, some coders might seek out jobs in specific manufacturing sectors that match their interests, such as sustainable goods or fashion. Environmentally conscious manufacturers work under special conditions and need workers, including coders, to have at least a little background in environmental science or justice. While one could write code for an automated, robotic solar panel without knowledge about solar power, the job will be much easier and more relevant if sustainability is a topic of interest to the coder. Similarly, coders who work on the manufacture of fashion items might choose to do so because they are interested in fashion in particular. For example, if a coder is working on a 3D-printed sneaker, she might have a better understanding of the style, materials, and shape of a sneaker if she has a background in fashion. Before taking a job in manufacturing, it is important that a coder think about the specific sector he or she is considering, and why it may or may not be a good fit.

CHALLENGES IN THE INDUSTRY

Coding in the manufacturing industry sounds like a fun experience—you get to work with new products, innovative technologies, and solutions that can benefit people. However, the industry does have its own challenges, though most of them are manageable if given a little forethought.

The manufacturing industry is made up primarily of for-profit companies. These companies are run by top executives who have various teams, managers, and employees working under them. Companies can be huge, sometimes numbering in the tens or hundreds of thousands of staff!

With the rise of online shopping, huge warehouses and fulfillment centers, like one of Amazon's pictured here, have begun to dot the land outside cities in the United States, as well as across the globe.

Think of Nike, General Electric, or Volkswagen. When coding for a manufacturer of this scale, there are several special considerations to keep in mind. First, though some companies are innovative, most have very specific needs and desires. A robotic arm may need to be coded to do a specific task. This is a fun project—until it is the only project, and until it drags on for months. A corporation can squash both the creativity and creative control of the coder. Most manufacturers have clear-cut objectives and need clear-cut solutions. For some coders, this is just fine, but for others, it can be a challenge.

Additionally, one must always consider the idea of intellectual property when working with a major manufacturer. Though a coder may write an amazing software program that controls a virtual reality device used on the factory floor, it may ultimately be the property of the company, rather than the coder. The coder, who takes home a respectable salary, will ultimately make less money than the corporation will make on the finished product. Likewise, the coder may be contractually obligated to avoid making similar products for other companies in the future. This can be frustrating for the coder, but profitable for the company.

Another aspect of manufacturing that is both frustrating for coders and great for companies is contract, or freelance, work. Some coders who have special skills in specific, and sometimes rare, computer languages are hired as contractors, rather than full-time employees. They are paid a set rate for

SCRATCH!

Some people enter the computer programming field hoping they will make money while working for a for-profit company. Coders can make large salaries with for-profits, but some are choosing nonprofits instead.

Nonprofit coding jobs come with salaries, but instead of supporting technical innovation for companies that produce goods, they focus on services. One example is the MIT Media Lab, an academic lab that has students and professors working together to create innovative programs. The MIT Media Lab created Scratch, a wildly popular visual programming language meant primarily for children. These researchers created an entirely new computer language, but they don't profit off of it! Instead, the language is used in schools and clubs, and through an open-source internet

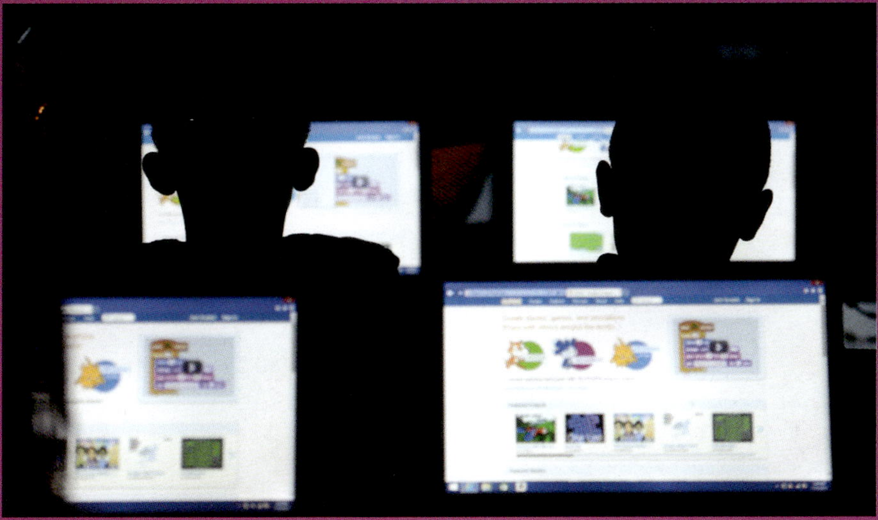

These kids use Scratch in a summer algebra class.

program. Its visual interface gets kids excited about coding their own projects. Since its launch in 2007, over forty million projects have been shared on the Scratch website.

their work, but lack the insurance benefits and job security that full-time employees earn. They also have to keep track of their own taxes, because they are not automatically taken out of their pay. Contract work can be lucrative, and it offers the flexibility to move from job to job, but it isn't for everyone. Coders should think about their ideal working conditions before taking any manufacturing job.

GENDER GAP

Whether you attend a four-year college, complete a two-year degree, or get a certificate from a coding bootcamp, you can become a coder. There are job options at all educational levels, as long as one is willing to work hard and learn the "foreign languages" of computers. It's easy to get started with coding. You can choose from various free coding games or classes online. It's just a click away! But if it's that easy, why doesn't it seem like everyone is becoming a coder?

The truth is, for much of the general population, there are still barriers to working in the coding field. For young women, it can be difficult to picture oneself in an industry that is dominated by men. According to the National Center for Women & Information Technology, even though women received 57 percent of all bachelor's degrees in 2012, they only received 18 percent of all computer and information science bachelor's degrees. And while women hold 57 percent of professional occupations in the United

Diversity of all types is important to have in any industry, and coding is no exception.

States, they only hold 26 percent of professional computing occupations. These numbers are far from equal. When women don't see themselves as computer programming leaders and professors, they are much less likely to pursue these paths.

This is where clubs and organizations come in. There are many nonprofits working hard to encourage girls in science, engineering, math, and science, and there are several that are focusing on coding. Girls Who Code offers events and clubs. Black Girls Code targets African American girls who might not otherwise have the opportunity to learn coding because of the gender and ethnicity gaps in the workplace, but also because of under-resourced schools and programs that simply don't offer the coding programs that children need, want, and deserve. Work is being done in this area, but there is still a long way to go.

Students at The Young Women's Leadership School of Astoria, an all-girls STEM-focused public school, listen to instructions during a coding class.

chapter_05

Get Coding

Now is the time to start thinking about a future in computer programming. As more and more companies turn to robotics, AI, 3D printing, and other technologies to transform their factories, coders will be needed every step of the way. If you have ever thought to yourself, "How is a website built?" or "Could I make my own app?" you might want to look into coding. In fact, if you've ever used an app, browsed a website, or purchased a product, you might want to look into coding! It touches so many aspects of our lives, and there are tons of opportunities for you to get involved right now.

CODE RIGHT NOW

No matter if you're in middle school or high school, you can jump right in when it comes to coding. If you've ever thought about learning a new language, Python or C++ are options! Learning to code is just like learning a language: you can start anytime, anywhere, even if you don't have a strong background in computers. In fact, earlier is better, because a young mind is best at learning and understanding languages.

So, how do you get involved? Start by looking for computer programming classes at school. There might be one that is called Coding, or it might be more specific, like an

At a code bootcamp, such as this one in Albuquerque, New Mexico, you might work together with other students to solve fun and interesting problems.

AutoCAD class that is connected to the shop department, or a robotics elective. Your school might have other classes that will get you comfortable with computers, like keyboarding or web design. It doesn't hurt to take another foreign language or math class, either, because those classes work similar parts of the brain and keep a person's language-learning skills sharp. Math classes are especially helpful if you want to work on coding for analytic programs.

Outside of class, you might want to join a coding club. These can be a super fun way to meet new people and learn to code at the same time. Ask around at school to learn if a coding club or LEGO robotics club is available. The local library, YMCA, YWCA, or similar youth organization might also have a coding club available. There are open clubs where anyone can join, but there are also special groups for girls, African American students, and others who are underrepresented in coding careers. Girlswhocode.com and Blackgirlscode.com can help you find one of these clubs near you.

AFTER GRADUATION

Once you've graduated high school, it will be time to move on to your next step. Do you want to go to a university? Community college? Somewhere else? When it comes to computer programming, there's a world of options, and plenty of jobs! Computer programming is a career track that

Just like other classes, coding courses have instructors who give lectures, show examples, and help you learn the language. This teacher is instructing an introduction to computer science class at a school in Colorado.

continues to grow. If you decide to go to college to learn to code, there will probably be plenty of well-paying jobs for you after college graduation.

Today, many employers prefer to hire programmers who have four-year college degrees, so it might be best to go to a university or college where you can earn a bachelor's degree. While there typically aren't degrees offered in coding, specifically, you could learn all about computer programming through a degree in information technology, information systems, computer science, or software engineering. Computer science is a very broad and popular field, and it usually includes some exposure to coding languages.

In addition to different focus areas, there are also two types of bachelor's degree programs to choose from. You could choose a Bachelor of Science (BS) degree, in which you learn computer programming concepts as well as the math and science behind them. Your school might also offer a Bachelor of Arts (BA) program in computer science, which would focus more on general education, with a little less math and science. Don't be afraid to ask college counselors about the different BA and BS offerings, as well as the focus areas. You should spend plenty of time considering the track that is the best fit for you. People end up in computer science through many different avenues and interests. There is no one correct way to become a coder.

If you do decide to get a BS or BA in computer science, there are many courses you can expect to take. You may dive into a computer networks course that teaches you how to solve problems related to internet security and access, or you could learn about the relationship between computer hardware and software in a computer architecture class. An algorithms course will teach you all the key components of algorithm design and analysis. Worried about paying for college? Many universities offer special scholarships just for computer science students!

Some people choose to complete a two-year degree instead of a bachelor's. This degree is called an associate's degree. It can cost less money, take less time, and be more

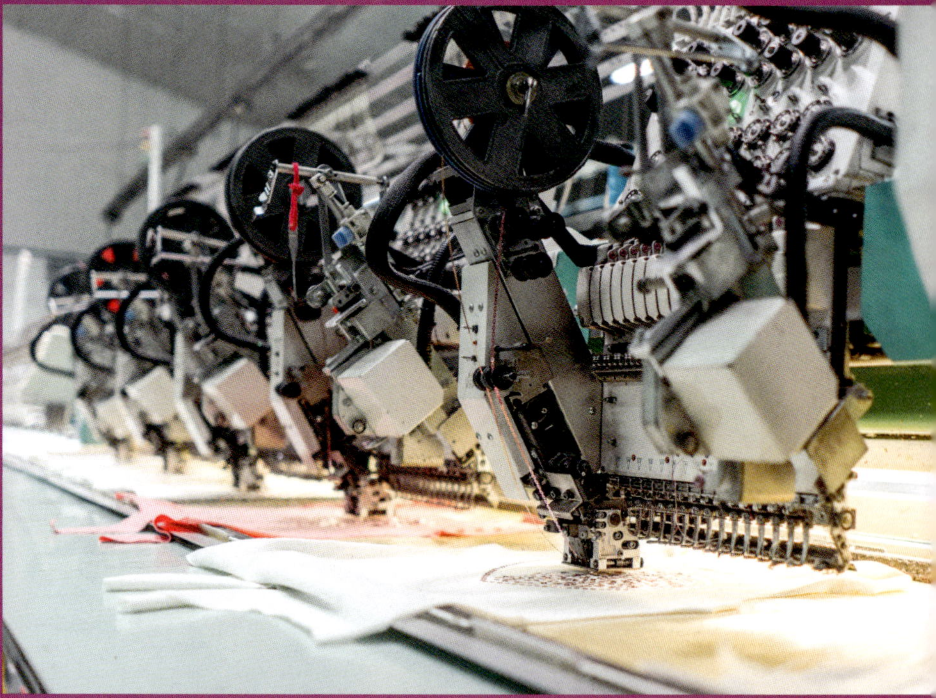

Unlike the 1800s power loom, these embroidery machines work entirely on their own!

CODING YOUR CLOTHES

Who said fashion and coding don't mix? If you want a job in the fashion industry, one way to get on the fast track to fashion success is through computer programming. Many people don't realize it, but clothing companies need coders on their staff, especially if they produce knitwear like sweaters and T-shirts. Many stores today are in the business of fast fashion. Companies like Forever21 and Zara produce new designs on a constant basis. Coders are needed to program the machines that actually make the clothing. And they need to be fast, because the stores want to keep up with trends! One day, a coder might produce a green sweater in an oversize fit. The next week, it will be a crop top! If you have an eye for fashion and a love for computer languages, there is room for you at many major fashion brands.

convenient for people who want to move quickly into the field. An associate's degree prepares students for entry-level information technology positions. Have you ever wondered who is in charge of the computer system at the local library, at school, or even in a business? It's probably someone with an IT degree. Two-year programs give students the skills they need in programming languages, databases, web applications, debugging, and more. You can take a class in Java, programming fundamentals, C++, and introductory work like an introduction to computing course. After getting a two-year degree, you can choose to move on to a bachelor's at a later date by transferring your credits to a different school. Then it should just take two to three years to complete your bachelor's degree.

KEEPING YOUR SKILLS

Whether you decide to go to a two-year college, to a four-year university, or on another track altogether, you will want to keep your coding skills up-to-date. Computer science is a field that is constantly changing as technology evolves and advances. Eventually, you may want to earn a certification in a specific programming language. You earn these by taking exams that test your knowledge of the language. These are offered by companies and schools, and can help you get hired or promoted.

Someday, you might also consider going to graduate school to earn a master's degree. While there is no specific computer programming degree at that level, you could get a master's in computer science, which would require courses in math, AI, and computer systems. As a master's student, you would probably choose a focus area, like algorithms or software development. In order to obtain your degree, you might have to complete a final project. Ultimately, that project could lead to a future business or job prospect. The sky is the limit when it comes to coding.

If you choose coding as a career path—and you love it—you may want to consider giving back to future generations by becoming a mentor, teacher, or tutor. All of those instructors at a coding club or coding event are professional coders who are giving their time and sharing their skills to teach kids and teens just like you. Someday, you will have the chance to give back through a nonprofit, or you could even start your own. Mentoring and teaching others are great ways to practice your skills and feel good at the same time.

BOOTCAMP

If you aren't ready to dive into a computer science major just yet, don't worry. Many people pursue other career tracks, like business, teaching, or the arts, and decide later on in life that they want to make a switch into the exciting world

Coding bootcamps, like Code Chrysalis in Japan, give learners the opportunity to turn a hobby into a career.

of programming. They might want to learn new things, make more money, or have more job flexibility. Fortunately, there are all sorts of options for those who want to learn coding outside of traditional higher education.

You may have heard of coding bootcamps like Flatiron School, AppAcademy, or Bloc. There are a lot of programs out there that range from online-only to in-person bootcamps that last from ten weeks to a year. In as little as three months, you can go through a full-time program that will teach you the ins and outs of one or more coding languages, as well as the basics of programming. Though most of these programs cost money, some don't require payment until you've landed a full-time job in programming. Their effectiveness is yet undecided, but bootcamps continue to gain popularity in major US cities. It seems that more and more people are interested in pursuing a career in coding, through traditional and untraditional means. If you would like to become a coder in the manufacturing industry, you can rest assured that jobs will be plentiful, new innovations will enter the market, and you will have plenty of opportunities to hone your skills in the years ahead.

Glossary

additive manufacturing Using 3D model data to build objects with layer upon layer of material.

algorithm A process followed by a computer in order to solve a problem.

application A program, such as an email program or a web browser, that has a specific use.

assembly line A method of arranging workers or machines in a factory so that each one completes a specific part of the product.

associate's degree A degree one receives after completing a two-year course of study, usually at a community college or a junior college.

augmented reality (AR) An enhanced view of reality in which a computer-generated image coexists with the user's real view.

automated Having been converted to an automatic process or processes.

autonomous Something that is capable of operating without human interaction.

bachelor's degree A degree one receives after completing a four-year course of study.

bootcamp A short, intensive course of training.

certification An official document that verifies a person's status, achievement, or qualification.

cloud A global network of servers that remotely host and deliver information and applications through an internet connection.

code Instructions written in a programming language that are then read and carried out by a computer.

computer-aided design (CAD) Software used to design products through 2D drawings or 3D models.

consumption The purchase and use of goods and services.

generative design A program's ability to generate outputs that meet specific constraints.

industrial Relating to factories and industry.

intellectual property Creations of the human mind that are protected by law from unauthorized use by others.

machine learning (ML) The study of algorithms and models that give systems the ability to learn and improve their performance independently of human action.

manufacturing An industry that is involved with producing objects on a large scale.

memoir A written account of the past, usually involving personal experiences.

model A representation of a proposed object.

nanotechnology Technology that deals with structures smaller than one hundred nanometers.

predictive maintenance Techniques that help tell when maintenance might be needed.

production The process of creating something, often from raw materials.

programmer A professional who writes instructions for computer programs.

programming language A formal language that instructs a computer or computing device to perform a task or create an output.

prototype The first example or model of a future product.

software A program used by a computer.

supply chain The system of processes that work in a sequence to produce and distribute a product.

virtual reality (VR) An artificial environment generated by a computer that sounds, feels, and looks like reality.

Further Information

BOOKS

McCully, Emily Arnold. *Dreaming in Code: Ada Byron Lovelace, Computer Pioneer*. Somerville, MA: Candlewick Press, 2019.

Moritz, Jeremy. *Code for Teens: The Awesome Beginner's Guide to Programming*. Herndon, VA: Mascot Books, 2018.

Powell, Asher. *Cool Careers Without College for People Who Love Coding*. Cool Careers Without College. New York: Rosen Publishing, 2018.

Vaidyanathan, Sheena. *Creative Coding in Python: 30+ Programming Projects in Art, Games, and More*. Beverly, MA: Quarry Books, 2018.

Young Rewired State. *Get Coding! Learn HTML, CSS & Javascript and Build a Website, App, and Game*. Somerville, MA: Candlewick Press, 2017.

WEBSITES

CODE COMBAT

https://codecombat.com

Learn coding while playing a real game. You can play Code Combat at school or at home.

KHAN ACADEMY: COMPUTER PROGRAMMING

https://www.khanacademy.org/computing/computer-programming

This free, comprehensive website walks you through basic and advanced lessons in computer programming.

SCRATCH

https://scratch.mit.edu

Use this simple code site to create your own animations, games, and more.

ORGANIZATIONS

BLACK GIRLS CODE

http://www.blackgirlscode.com

This organization hosts coding programs and events across the country!

CHICKTECH

https://chicktech.org

This organization supports women and girls in tech through events, workshops, and conferences.

CODE.ORG

https://code.org

This nonprofit works to encourage coding education in and out of schools.

CODER DOJO

https://coderdojo.com

Click over to CoderDojo to find free coding clubs in your area.

GIRLS WHO CODE

https://girlswhocode.com

Check out the nationwide movement that is dedicated to closing the gender gap in technology.

#YESWECODE

http://www.yeswecode.org

This nationwide initiative strives to bring tech opportunities to underrepresented young people.

BIBLIOGRAPHY

Barnhorn, Alexis. "60 Years of CAD Infographic: The History of CAD Since 1957." Part Solutions. Accessed November 11, 2018. https://partsolutions.com/60-years-of-cad-infographic-the-history-of-cad-since-1957.

Cohn, David. "Evolution of Computer-Aided Design." Digital Engineering 247, December 1, 2010. https://www.digitalengineering247.com/article/evolution-of-computer-aided-design.

Columbus, Louis. "10 Ways Cloud Computing Will Drive Manufacturing Growth in 2018." Manufacturing.Net, February 23, 2018. https://www.manufacturing.net/article/2018/02/10-ways-cloud-computing-will-drive-manufacturing-growth-2018.

Dishman, Lydia. "Why Coding Is Still the Most Important Job Skill of the Future." Fast Company, June 14, 2016. https://www.fastcompany.com/3060883/why-coding-is-the-job-skill-of-the-future-for-everyone.

Florentine, Sharon. "The 10 Best Coding Bootcamps." CIO, October 22, 2018. https://www.cio.com/article/3222718/it-skills-training/the-10-best-coding-bootcamps.html.

Forbes Technology Council. "Considering a New Job? Here Are 10 Industries in Need of Programmers." Forbes, October 18, 2017. https://www.forbes.com/

sites/forbestechcouncil/2017/10/18/considering-a-new-job-here-are-10-industries-in-need-of-programmers/#655f10445fe3.

Foremski, Rom. "Mind the Gap: AI and Machine Learning Lag in Adoption." ZDNet, December 2, 2018. https://www.zdnet.com/article/mind-the-gap-ai-and-machine-learning-lag-in-adoption.

Fraga, Alberto Iglesias. "This 3D Printer Could One Day Make New Body Parts for Transplant Patients." Business Insider, October 9, 2018. https://www.businessinsider.com/this-3d-printer-could-make-new-organs-for-transplant-patients-2018-10.

Genota, Lauraine. "K–12 Dealmaking: Girls Who Code Expands to Canada; Catapult Learning Makes Acquisition." EdWeek Market Brief, November 15, 2018. https://marketbrief.edweek.org/marketplace-k-12/k-12-dealmaking-girls-who-code-canada-kinvolved-photomath-yuanfudao.

"Girls in IT: The Facts Infographic." National Center for Women and Information Technology. Accessed November 10, 2018. https://www.ncwit.org/infographic/3435.

Heilweil, Rebecca. "Eyes and Ears 3D-Printed from Flesh Could Boost Our Senses." Wired, November 20, 2018. https://www.wired.com/story/3d-printed-flesh-body-parts.

Howitt, Doran. "Computer-Aided Design for All." *InfoWorld*. December 3, 1984. 38–39.

Huang, Roger. "How to Get a Job Working with Artificial Intelligence/Machine Learning." The Next Web, December 1, 2018. https://thenextweb.com/contributors/2018/11/30/how-to-get-a-job-working-with-artificial-intelligence-machine-learning.

Kim, Chloe. "For Early Participants of Girls Who Code, the Program's Impact is Indelible." EdScoop, April 30, 2018. https://edscoop.com/girls-who-code-graduates-computer-science-stem.

Kushmaro, Philip. "5 Ways Industrial AI is Revolutionizing Manufacturing." CIO, September 27, 2018. https://www.cio.com/article/3309058/manufacturing-industry/5-ways-industrial-ai-is-revolutionizing-manufacturing.html.

Lohr, Steve. "As Coding Boot Camps Close, the Field Faces a Reality Check." *New York Times*, August 24, 2017. https://www.nytimes.com/2017/08/24/technology/coding-boot-camps-close.html.

PricewaterhouseCoopers and Manufacturing Institute. "The Internet of Things: What it Means for US Manufacturing." February 2015. http://www.themanufacturinginstitute.org/Research/Disruptive-Innovations-in-Manufacturing/~/media/659a17245f6f4375bcce889079427cb6.ashx.

———. "The New Hire: How a New Generation of Robots is Transforming Manufacturing." September 2014. http://www.themanufacturinginstitute.org/Research/Disruptive-Innovations-in-Manufacturing/~/media/4A8E6F46F17A48D6A1CA03D800F7A2C0.ashx.

———. "Upskilling Manufacturing: How Technology is Disrupting America's Industrial Labor Force." June 2016. http://www.themanufacturinginstitute.org/Research/Disruptive-Innovations-in-Manufacturing/~/media/E9F0B41DEC4F40B6AE4D74CBC794D26D.ashx.

Peters, Adele. "These 3D-Printed Body Parts Let Surgeons Practice On a Model Before They Open You Up." Fast Company, October 4, 2018. https://www.fastcompany.com/90243319/these-3d-printed-body-parts-let-surgeons-practice-on-a-model-before-they-open-you-up.

Plantec, Peter. "The Fascinating Story of How AutoDesk Came to Be (Part 1)." StudioDaily, January 7, 2012. http://www.studiodaily.com/2012/01/the-fascinating-story-of-how-autodesk-came-to-be-part-1.

Rizwan, Omar. "A Snapshot of Programming Language History." Increment, April 2018. https://increment.com/programming-languages/language-history.

Robinson, Adam. "A Brief History of the American Manufacturing Industry + Infographic." The Rodon Group, February 22, 2016. https://www.rodongroup.com/blog/a-brief-history-of-the-american-manufacturing-industry-infographic.

———. "The Future is Now: Why These 5 Advanced Manufacturing Technologies Trends Will Dominate 2018." Cerasis. Accessed January 18, 2018. https://cerasis.com/2018/01/18/advanced-manufacturing-technologies.

———. "The History of Robotics in Manufacturing." Cerasis. Accessed October 6, 2018. https://cerasis.com/2014/10/06/robotics-in-manufacturing.

———. "How Can Technology Be the Game Changer for Your Manufacturing Business?" Cerasis. October 22, 2018. https://cerasis.com/2018/10/22/manufacturing-business.

Rosenberg, Tina. "A High-Paying Job? Go to App Boot Camp." *New York Times*, April 17, 2018. https://www.nytimes.com/2018/04/17/opinion/computer-science-boot-camp.html.

Roser, Christoph. *Faster, Better, Cheaper in the History of Manufacturing: From the Stone Age to Lean Manufacturing and Beyond*. New York: Productivity Press, 2016.

Vickery, Ben. "Five Technological Applications Impacting Manufacturing Innovation." NIST. May 24, 2016. https://www.nist.gov/blogs/manufacturing-innovation-blog/five-technological-applications-impacting-manufacturing.

"What Is Additive Manufacturing?" GE Additive. Accessed November 2, 2018. https://www.ge.com/additive/additive-manufacturing.

Williams, Nick. "Milwaukee Organizations Volunteer to Teach Coding to Local Students." *Milwaukee Business Journal*, December 7, 2018. https://www.bizjournals.com/milwaukee/news/2018/12/07/milwaukee-organizations-volunteer-to-teach-coding.html.

Winick, Erin. "I 3D-Printed Every Bit of My Wedding–Including My Bouquet." *MIT Technology Review*, November 30, 2018. https://www.technologyreview.com/s/612486/i-3-d-printed-every-bit-of-my-weddingincluding-my-bouquet.

INDEX

Page numbers in **boldface** refer to images.

additive manufacturing (AM), 35–36
  3D printing, 11, 19, **20**, 21, 23, 26, **34**, 35, 47, 55
algorithms, 8, 31, 59, 63
applications, 5–6, 10–11, 19, 26, 29, 33, 36, 55, 62
artificial intelligence (AI), 30–32
assembly lines, **9**, 19–21, 27, 30, 39, 44
augmented reality (AR), 38–39, 41
automation, 16, 19–20, 23, 25, 38, 44–45, 47
autonomous machines, 46
autonomous vehicles, 36–38

Black Girls Code, 53, 57

certification, 62
cloud computing, 32–33, 40, 45
code, definition, 5
coding, 6–7
  analytical processes, 24, 26–27
  in design, 17–19
  in fashion industry, 61
  in manufacturing, 9, 11, 13, 44–49,
  in production, 19–23, 30–33, 41, 45
  teaching, 63
computer-aided design (CAD), 10, **17**, 18, 21, 36, 40, **46**, 47
  AutoCAD, 10, 18, 21, 40, 57
  SketchUp, 18

degrees
  associate's degree, 59, 62
  bachelor's degree, 52, 58–59, 62
drones, 37-38, **37**

education
  bootcamps, 7, 47, 52, **56**, 63–65, **64**
  certifications, 52, 62
  college, 57–59, 62
  computer science, 45, 58–59, **58**, 62–63
  continuing education, 62–63
  graduate school, 63
  high school, 56–57
employment
  challenges, 48–49, 52
  nonprofits, 50–51
  opportunities, 43–48
  salaries, 45, 49–50
  specializing, 46–48
  underrepresented groups, 52–53, 57

generative design, 40, 47
Girls Who Code, 53, 57
Google Glass, **39**

Hanratty, Patrick J., 18

industrial centers, 22
Industrial Revolution, 14
intellectual property, 49
Internet of Things (IoT), 33–34

Lovelace, Ada, 7–8, **8**

machine learning (ML), 46–47
manufacturing
  consumption, 17
  history, 14–17, 43–44
  power loom, **15**
  worker retention 22, 25
Massachusetts Institute of Technology (MIT) 18, 50

nanotechnology, 34–35, 45
National Center for Women & Information Technology, 52

predictive maintenance, 30
programmers (coders), 7, 29–30, 43
  in analytical processes, 24, 26–27
  in design, 10, 17–19
  in fashion industry, 61
  history, 7–8
  in manufacturing, 9–11, 13, 17, 29–30, 43–44, 46–49, 52
  in production, 19–23, 30–33, 41, 45
programming languages, 5–9, 11, 15, 45–46, 49, 50, 56–58, 61–62, 64
prototypes 23, 35–36

radio-frequency identification (RFID), 16
robotics, 6, **6**, **9**, 11, **12**, 26–27, 32–33, 37, 44, 46–47, 49, 55, 57
  in artificial intelligence, 30–32, **31**
  in design, 19
  history, 15–16
  in production, 21

software, 5, 7, 10–11, 18–21, 23–24, 26–27, 36, 40, 49, 58–59, 63
smart manufacturing, 33–34
smartphones, **28**
supply chain, 31

3D models, 18, **20**, 21
3D printing, 11, 19, **20**, 21, 23, 26, **34**, 35, 47, 55
2D models, 18

virtual reality (VR), 38–39, 41, 49

Walker, John, 10

Young Women's Leadership School, The, **54**

ABOUT THE AUTHOR

Kaitlyn Duling believes in the power of words to change hearts, minds, and actions. An avid reader and writer who grew up in Illinois, she now resides in Washington, DC. She knows that knowledge of the past is the key to our future, and wants to ensure that all children and families have access to high-quality information. Duling has written over sixty books for children and teens. You can learn more about her at http://www.kaitlynduling.com.